LANDMARKS IN MY COMMUNITY

THE LIBRARY

BY SADIE SILVA

Gareth Stevens PUBLISHING

Please visit our website, www.garethstevens.com. For a free color catalog of all our high-quality books, call toll free 1-800-542-2595 or fax 1-877-542-2596.

Library of Congress Cataloging-in-Publication Data
Names: Silva, Sadie, author.
Title: The library / Sadie Silva.
Description: Buffalo, NY : Gareth Stevens, 2025. | Series: Landmarks in my community | Includes bibliographical references and index.
Identifiers: LCCN 2023034812 (print) | LCCN 2023034813 (ebook) | ISBN 9781538293133 (library binding) | ISBN 9781538293126 (paperback) | ISBN 9781538293140 (ebook)
Subjects: LCSH: Public libraries–Juvenile literature. | Libraries–Juvenile literature. | Librarians–Juvenile literature.
Classification: LCC Z665.5 .S57 2025 (print) | LCC Z665.5 (ebook) | DDC 027.4–dc23/eng/20230821
LC record available at https://lccn.loc.gov/2023034812
LC ebook record available at https://lccn.loc.gov/2023034813

Published in 2025 by
Gareth Stevens Publishing
2544 Clinton Street
Buffalo, NY 14224

Designer: Andrea Davison-Bartolotta
Editor: Caitie McAneney

Photo credits: Cover, p. 1 Wangkun Jia/Shutterstock.com; series art (page numbers) art_of_sun/Shutterstock.com; series art (map background) Marian Salabai/Shutterstock.com; p. 5 diignat/Shutterstock.com; p. 7 PeopleImages.com - Yuri A/Shutterstock.com; p. 9 Protasov AN/Shutterstock.com; pp. 11, 13 Tyler Olson/Shutterstock.com; p. 15 wavebreakmedia/Shutterstock.com; p. 17 Pixe1Power/Shutterstock.com; p. 19 Rawpixel.com/Shutterstock.com; p. 21 PK Studio/Shutterstock.com.

Printed in the United States of America

CPSIA compliance information: Batch #CS25GS: For further information contact Gareth Stevens, New York, New York at 1-800-542-2595.

CONTENTS

Boldface words appear in the glossary.

Finding Books

Imagine you want to learn about something new. Maybe it's an interesting animal or sport. Maybe you want to get lost in a story. Where can you go in your community to find books and **information**?

The Library!

You can visit the library! Most communities have libraries. Big cities have large libraries. Small towns may have smaller libraries. Schools usually have libraries too. They have books for people to **borrow** and computers for people to use.

A library is a building that holds many books and **materials**. Smaller libraries might have only one room. Bigger libraries may have many rooms and floors. They often have shelves with books of all kinds. Many have a computer **section**.

Visiting the Library

Anyone can visit a library! It's a public space. You need to get a library card to take books and materials home. Usually, you need to prove that you live in the community to get a library card.

Working at the Library

Librarians work at libraries. They order books and keep track of them. They know how to help people find certain information. They know a lot about books and computers. Librarians are community helpers!

What Happens There?

At the library, people can **browse** the books quietly. Some libraries also hold special events. They might have authors, **illustrators**, and speakers visit. Libraries may also have classes for kids and adults.

An Important Place

Libraries are important parts of any community. People can use books and computers at the library for free. This helps all kids stay on track with learning, no matter how much money their family has.

Libraries are also important gathering places. Students can meet in libraries to work together. People from the community can go to events. People might meet for book clubs or special groups. It's a safe space for people to come together.

Your Own Library

Have you ever been to your community's library? You can ask your parents to take you there. Discover new books. Ask librarians questions about books or their job. It may be the start of a new learning adventure!

GLOSSARY

borrow: To take something with the promise to return it.

browse: To look at things slowly.

illustrator: An artist who makes pictures for books.

information: Knowledge or facts that come from a source.

material: Something used for a purpose. In a library, materials include books, movies, magazines, and more.

section: Any part of a whole.

FOR MORE INFORMATION

BOOKS

Anderson, AnnMarie. *Meet a Librarian!* New York, NY: Children's Press, 2021.

Kawa, Katie. *A Day with a Librarian.* New York, NY: Cavendish Square Publishing, 2021.

WEBSITES

Library
kids.kiddle.co/Library
Explore more fun facts about libraries.

Library Careers: For Kids
www.ala.org/educationcareers/libcareers/kids
Would you like to be a librarian someday? Find out more about the job!

Publisher's note to educators and parents: Our editors have carefully reviewed these websites to ensure that they are suitable for students. Many websites change frequently, however, and we cannot guarantee that a site's future contents will continue to meet our high standards of quality and educational value. Be advised that students should be closely supervised whenever they access the internet.

INDEX